Hummingbirds

GEORGE K. PECK

SMART APPLE MEDIA

Published by

Smart Apple Media

123 South Broad Street

Mankato, Minnesota 56001

⚘

Copyright © 1998 Smart Apple Media.

Photos by George K. Peck,

Mark Peck,

Sid & Shirley Rucker, Mildred Ladyman / GeoImagery

Editorial assistance by Barbara Ciletti

Library of Congress Cataloging-in-Publication Data

Peck, George K.

Hummingbirds / written by George Peck.

p. cm.

Includes index.

Summary: An introduction to the physical characteristics, habits, and natural

environment of various species of hummingbirds.

ISBN 1-887068-09-0

1. Hummingbirds—Juvenile literature. [1. Hummingbirds.] I. Title.

QL696.A558P435 1998   96-19431

598.8'99—dc20   CIP

                                                                                    AC

First Edition   5 4 3 2 1

C O N T E N T S

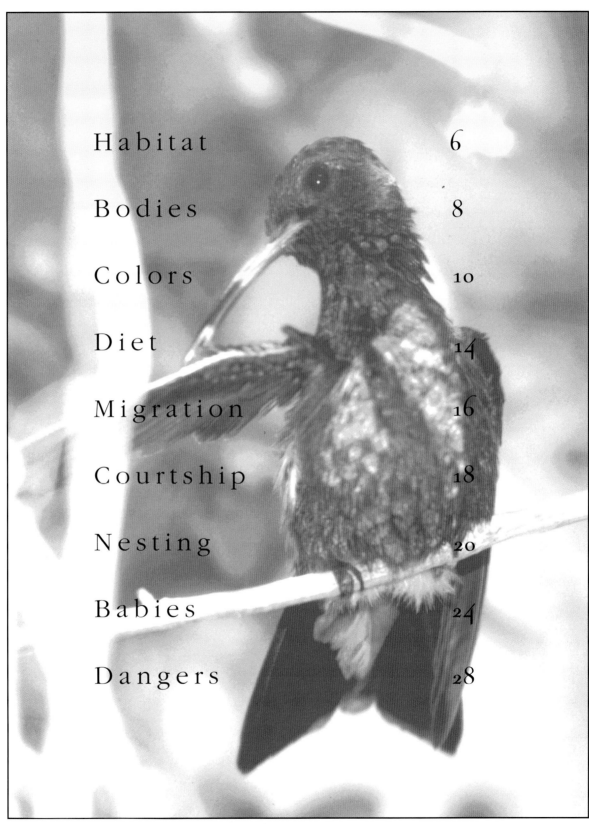

W

hen European explorers arrived in America, they found many strange new plants and animals. They saw herds of thunder-ing bison, trees that seemed to reach the clouds, and flocks of birds filled the sky.

Wherever they turned they saw something new.

One tiny creature, no larger than a man's thumb, amazed and enchanted them all. It flashed red and green and purple and blue, appearing and disappearing in a colorful blur. It flew up and down and backward and forward with a strange humming sound. It could hover in midair, its tiny wings a buzzing blur. They did not know what they were seeing. It seemed too small and fast to be a bird. Could it be some sort of moth? A fairy?

They had never before seen such a creature.

The ancient Mexicans compared the birds to the rays of the sun. The Portuguese called them "flower kissers." Today, some people call them "feathered jewels" for the way they fly and glitter in the sunlight. But most of us know them by their common name.

We call them hummingbirds.

There are 338 species of hummingbirds in the family Trochilidae. All of them live in North, Central, and South America. Most types of hummingbirds live in tropical areas, where flowers bloom all year long.

Hummingbirds can be found as far north as Alaska or as far south as the tip of South America. Only twenty-three different kinds of hummingbirds live north of Mexico, with four venturing into Canada. Hummingbirds have adapted to a variety of environments, from lush rain forest to dry desert regions.

One species, called the Giant Hummingbird, is found in the Andes Mountains as high as 15,000 feet (4570 m) above sea level. Costa's Hummingbird prefers the driest of climates and lives in the desert areas along the coast of California and in the southwestern United States. The Rufous Hummingbird can be found in meadows above the treeline in the subarctic. It is the only hummingbird to venture as far north as Alaska.

Of the 23 species known to visit the United States and Canada, 22 are found west of the Rocky Mountains, mostly in the warmer regions of Southern California and Arizona.

The Ruby-throated Hummingbird has an exclusive range. In the northern United States and Canada, it is the only hummingbird regularly found east of the Rocky Mountains. During the summer, the Ruby-throated Hummingbird is common in woodlands and gardens from Texas to Florida, throughout the midwestern and the northeastern states, and up into southern Canada.

Costa's Hummingbird perched on a branch.

The smallest of all living birds is a species of hummingbird—the Bee Hummingbird. The tiny Bee Hummingbird lives in Cuba. It is 2 1/4 inches (6 cm) long—smaller than some insects! The largest of all hummingbirds, the Giant Hummingbird of the Andes Mountains, measures about 8 1/2 inches (22 cm) from head to tail. That's almost as big as a robin.

All of the hummingbirds found in the United States and Canada are between 3 and 5 inches (8 and 13 cm) long, with wingspans of about 4 inches (10 cm). The Ruby-throated Hummingbird, our most widespread and common species, is 3 1/2 inches (9 cm) long and weighs 1/10 of an ounce (3 g), about the same as one copper penny.

You will never see a hummingbird walking or hopping. Their feet are built for perching on small twigs or branches. When a hummer needs to get from one place to another, it flies.

Hummingbirds have long bills that help them reach deep into flower blossoms. Most hummingbird bills are 1 to 2 inches (2.5 to 5 cm) long, but some hummingbirds, such as the Andean Swordbill, can have bills up to 4 inches (10 cm) in length. The long bill helps the swordbill reach into the deep flower tube of a certain type of passion flower, whose nectar is its favorite food.

Hummingbirds are remarkable flyers and great fun to watch. They can hover as though they are hanging in the air. They can easily fly backward and straight up and down. Some of the smaller birds' wings move as swiftly as 200 beats per second—much too fast for your eyes to see. Their wings beat so fast that they make a humming sound, which is why we call them "hummingbirds."

Because hummingbirds are so small, cold weather can be very dangerous to them. Their tiny bodies lose heat quickly when the temperature falls. During cold spells or chilly nights, when a hummingbird can't keep itself warm by feeding and flying, it will perch on a sheltered branch, fluff up its feathers, and go into a state of torpor. The hummer's heart beats slower, its body temperature drops, and its breathing slows. Torpor is similar to hibernation. It is the hummingbird's way of conserving energy. It might last for a day, or for only a few hours. In the morning, or when the weather warms up, the hummer slowly awakens. It absorbs heat from the sun, or creates its own heat by vibrating its wings. As soon as it has warmed up, the hummer heads for the nearest flower to feed.

Hummingbirds are often called feathered jewels, and it's easy to see why. Their feathers actually appear to sparkle and shimmer like emeralds, rubies, and amethysts. As you watch a hummingbird move, its colors may appear to change. Some of the hummer's feathers are iridescent. Like oil floating on water, they can reflect a rainbow of colors. The throat of a Ruby-throated Hummingbird might appear greenish, or bronze, or black, but when the sun hits the throat feathers just right, they blaze ruby red. Feathers that looked gold a moment ago may turn to green or blue.

In most species, the male hummers are more colorful than the females, and their colors are brightest during the mating season. Males may use their dazzling plumage to attract their mates.

Many hummers are named after the color of their feathers. The male Ruby-throat has a bronze-green back and grayish white chest and belly, but his most outstanding feature is his throat, which is a brilliant metallic red. The male Blue-throated Hummingbird, one of the largest North American hummers, has a bright blue throat and dark bluish gray tail feathers with white on the tips. The bright metallic green Berylline Hummingbird is named after the beryl, a green gemstone. The male Violet-crowned Hummingbird of Mexico has a violet-colored head with a greenish-bronze back and tail.

Even though hummingbirds are tiny, they have big appetites. That's because they fly almost constantly and their wings beat very rapidly. The heart rate of hummers is as high as 1,260 beats per minute. They burn up energy quickly, so they need to eat a lot of food. In fact, they may eat and drink more than eight times their body weight each day.

The main source of food for all hummingbirds is nectar. Nectar is a kind of thin, sweet syrup found in the blossoms of most flowers. Nectar is loaded with sugars and other nutrients. The hummers use their long bills and their even longer tongues to probe deep into the flower blossoms. They feed by moving their tongues rapidly in and out of the nectar, the way a cat drinks water from a bowl. But hummingbirds are much faster than cats—their pointed tongues lap up nectar at 13 licks per second!

The hummer's ability to hover is very important for feeding. Most nectar flowers don't offer a place to perch, and the bird must eat while hovering in midair.

Hummingbirds can be very fussy about what types of flowers they like. Some species have very long or very short beaks that make it easier to drink the nectar from certain types of blossoms. Flower color is also important. The Ruby-throated Hummingbird prefers to visit red and orange flowers, and it will often fly right past blue flowers without bothering to taste their nectar. For some reason, the color red is a big favorite of the Ruby-throat. If you are wearing a red cap in the garden, you might find a hummer buzzing around your head, wondering how to get to the nectar.

Hummingbirds also eat small insects that they find in and near flowers. Their tongues have a feathery fringe that lets them hold onto the insects.

When there are not enough flowers in bloom, some hummingbird species may feed on other plant juices. The Ruby-throated Hummingbird has a special association with a woodpecker called the Yellow-bellied Sapsucker. A sapsucker will drill hundreds of holes in a tree trunk. Sweet sap flows from the holes. The sapsucker feeds on the sap and on the insects that are attracted to it. In the early spring, when very few flower blossoms are available, Ruby-throated Hummingbirds will also feed on the sugary sap.

Because hummers must have blossoms to feed on, all hummingbirds that live and breed in the northern United States and in Canada must migrate south for the winter. Some hummers spend their winters in the southern states, but most fly farther south into Mexico or Central America, where the weather is warmer and there is an unlimited supply of nectar.

But how can such tiny birds fly such great distances? For many years, people thought that hummingbirds hitchhiked south on the backs of migrating geese. We now know that this is not true. Hummingbirds are strong fliers. They can reach speeds of up to 41 miles per hour (66 kph). As remarkable as it seems, the Ruby-throated Hummingbird makes a nonstop flight across the Gulf of Mexico, more than 500 miles (800 km), on its own tiny wings.

But the grand champion of hummingbird migration is the reddish-brown Rufous Hummingbird. It flies up to 2,500 miles every spring and fall, from Alaska all the way to Central America.

Not all hummingbird species migrate. Many tropical species, such as the Buff-bellied Hummingbird of Mexico and southern Texas, live where flowers bloom all year long. They might travel a short distance in the spring and fall, but they remain in the same general area their entire lives.

Buff-bellied Hummingbird in flight.

The male hummer begins its migration to summer habitats before the female and chooses its breeding territory immediately upon arrival. The male Ruby-throated Hummingbird usually picks a spot in a wooded area, but it may choose any place that offers lots of flowering plants, such as a garden or a park. The male will fiercely defend his territory from other males, attacking with his beak and claws if necessary. You might not think that a little hummingbird would be all that scary, but imagine how long that sharp 1-inch beak looks to a 3-inch-long hummer!

Once the female arrives, the male tries to attract her by swooping back and forth, wings buzzing, making loud, high-pitched calls. Hummingbird voices may sound like a mouse, or a squeaking wheel. They use their voices mostly during courtship, or when attacking rival hummingbirds. Sometimes the female will join the male in these aerial courtship displays.

Different hummers have different courtship flights. The Allen's Hummingbird of California does a spectacular power dive from a height of about 60 feet (18 m) and reaches a speed of about 63 miles per hour (101 kph). Just before he hits the ground, he spreads his tail feathers and pulls up, making a loud ripping sound.

After mating, the male Ruby-throated Hummingbird leaves the building of the nest to the female. She often chooses to build her nest in areas that allow her a good view of her surroundings. Hummingbirds sometimes reuse old nests, but more often than not they build new ones.

The female hummer carefully attends to all of the details of construction by herself. Using lichen, bark pieces, and fine grasses, she takes seven to ten days to build her tiny nest. The inside of the nest is lined with soft, cottony plant fibers. The outside is covered with bits of lichen and bark held in place with strands of spiderweb.

Many different types of trees can be selected to hold the new nest, but Ruby-throated Hummingbirds prefer those with lichen-covered bark because it will camouflage the nest. The finished nest, about the size of a walnut, looks just like another small knot on the branch.

When the nest is finished, the female lays two tiny white eggs about 1/2 inch (1.3 cm) long. That's about the size of a small jellybean. The female sits on her eggs for 15 to 16 days. Her body heat keeps the eggs nice and warm so that the baby hummingbirds inside the eggs grow quickly.

The eggs and nest of the Ruby-throated Hummingbird.

Baby hummers are born blind, helpless, naked, and about the size of a bumblebee when they hatch. After a few days, pinfeathers or feather sheathes appear on the baby hummingbirds' bodies. Inside these sheathes, tiny, soft feathers are growing. Their final feathers quickly emerge from the white "pins."

Since they can't feed themselves, their mother stands on the edge of the nest to feed her babies nectar and small insects that she gathers and stores in her crop, which is a food pouch in her throat. She transfers this mixture to the babies by putting her long bill into their throats. Then she pumps the food from her crop to their stomachs.

The babies grow so rapidly that their bodies are too big for the nest after their first week. Fortunately, the hummingbird nest is designed to expand. The movement of the baby hummers stretches the spiderweb and plant fibers. The nest gets bigger and the babies keep growing.

Both babies are ready to leave the nest after three weeks. As a matter of fact, they're bulging out of it. They stand on the edge of the nest and flap their wings with vigor; they can actually lift off the nest for a few moments. Their mother may or may not be around when that first "flight" takes place. Young hummers instinctively know how to fly. As soon as their feathers are fully developed, they take off!

Many young hummers look a lot like their mothers during the first year. For example, the male Ruby-throat doesn't get his full iridescent red throat until the following spring when he has grown to full adulthood.

Two broods are often raised in a season. Sometimes nests can be destroyed by storms or squirrels, so the adult hummers just start over with mating and building a nest. A third brood may be raised if time permits.

Breeding and raising hummingbird families is very important to the survival of the species. Hummers often live for only a year or two. There are exceptions of course. A Blue-throated Hummingbird was known to have lived for 12 years in captivity, and one Planalto Hermit was known to have reached the ripe old age of 14. Captive birds do tend to live longer than birds in the wild because they simply don't face the same dangers.

D A N G E R S

Although hummers live peacefully with many songbirds, large mammals, and people, they do have enemies. For instance, domestic cats, if they get the chance, can intercept a hummer in midflight. Adult hummers may be hunted by small hawks, and the smaller hummers sometimes make a meal for a praying mantis.

On one occasion, a largemouth bass was seen to have leaped right out of the water and swallow a hummer whole. Hummers can also get caught in spider webs, window screens, and the spines of thistles. Young hummingbirds still in the nest may be attacked by squirrels or other birds.

Migration is a very dangerous time for these fragile little birds. Flying long distances uses up a lot of energy and makes hummingbirds more vulnerable to predators, disease, and changes in the weather. Storms, high winds, and sudden cold snaps kill thousands of hummers every year.

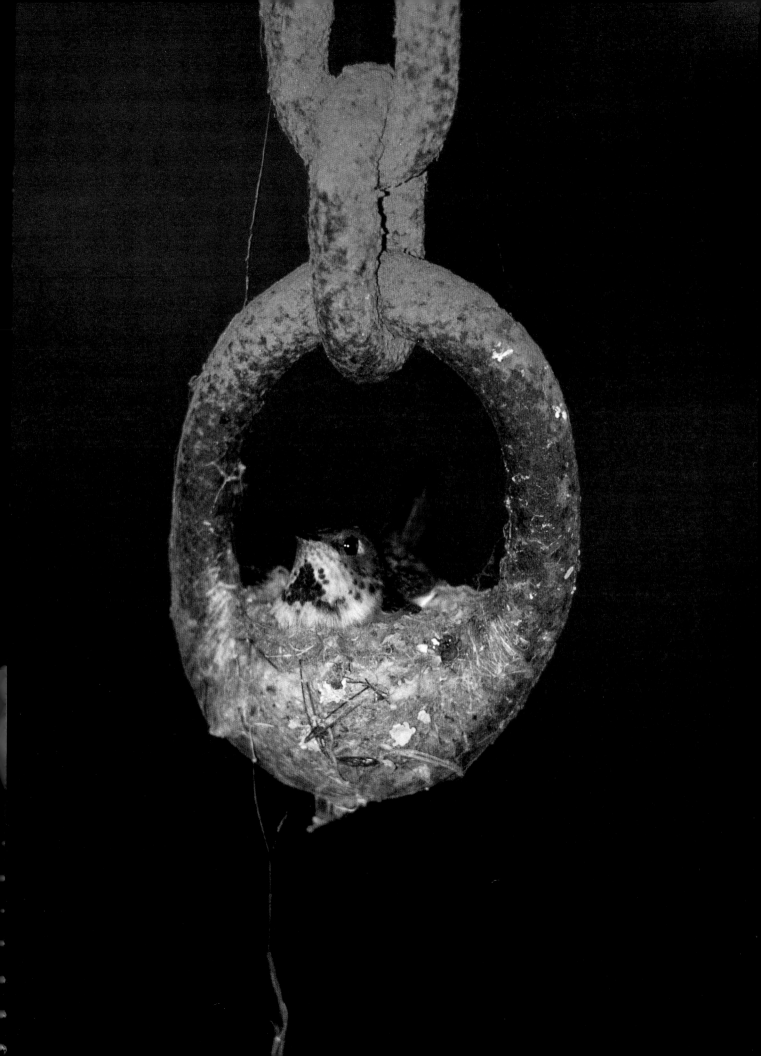

Hummingbirds need flowers, but flowers need hummingbirds too. When a hummingbird moves from one flower to another, it carries tiny bits of pollen stuck to its beak and head. The pollen is transferred from flower to flower. This makes it possible for the flowers to make seeds and create new plants. Without hummingbirds and other pollinators, many flowering plants could not survive.

Hummingbirds are common throughout the United States and southern Canada, but they are so small and fast that you might not notice them. To attract hummingbirds to your home, you can hang a special hummingbird feeder filled with sugar water. Better yet, you can plant lots of flowers such as hollyhocks, columbine, and petunias. Hummers prefer the red and orange varieties. A well-tended flower garden will attract plenty of hummers, and you'll also get lots of butterflies.

Whether you call them feathered jewels, flower kissers, or just plain hummingbirds, watching these amazing birds buzz from flower to flower is a wonderful summer pastime.

INDEX